IS THERE
SEX AFTER 40?

By: Toni Goffe

First published in Great Britain
by Pendulum Gallery Press

Manufactured in the United States of America

30 29 28 27 26 25 24 23 22 21 20 19 18 17 16 15 14 13 12 11 10 9 8 7 6 5 4 3 2 1

BOSTON AMERICA C★O★R★P
125 Walnut St., P.O. Box 9132, Watertown, MA 02272-9132
Telephone #: (617) 923-1111   Fax #: (617) 923-8839

-"I REMEMBER WHEN THE ONLY THING YOU WANTED TO TAKE TO BED WAS **ME**!"-

" OH, HELLO DEAR, I DIDN'T KNOW YOU WERE INTERESTED IN PHOTOGRAPHY......" -

"WHERE DID YOU COME FROM? I'M NOT DOING CAR POOL
TILL NEXT WEEK!"—

-"IT'S ALL RIGHT DAD, I'M JUST KEEPING MY HOMEWORK DRY!"-

"OH NO! THEY'RE AT IT AGAIN!"

" - YOU KNOW WHAT I MISS ZELDA, THE CHILDREN'S LAUGHTER!" -

"YES, I KNOW WE'RE SEPARATED, BUT HE KEEPS COMING BACK TO APOLOGIZE!!" -

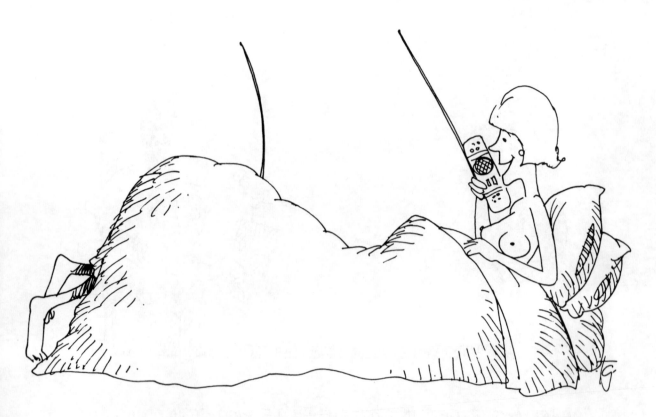

-"KEEP A'COMIN' BIG DADDY, YOU'RE RIGHT ON TARGET!"-

" WHAT ABOUT GETTING TO THE LITTLE PIGGY THAT HAS
TO GET UP EARLY AND GO TO WORK TOMORROW!"-

"GEORGE, BE GENTLE WITH ME...."-

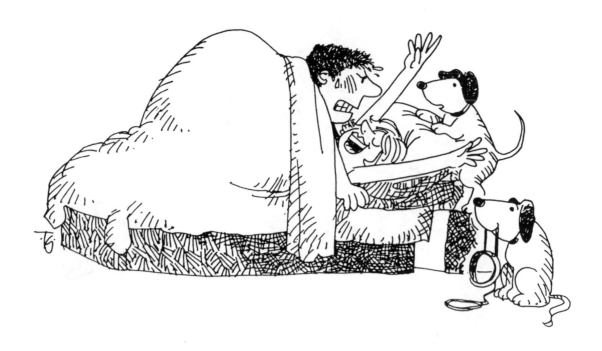

" NOT NOW, RUFUS, ... NOT **NOW!** " -

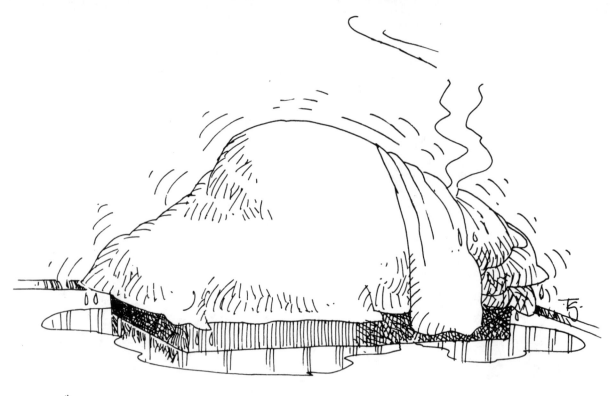

" JOHN, I THINK THE ELECTRIC BLANKET IS STILL SWITCHED ON...."-

"- ANDREA, WILL YOU STOP LEVITATING AND COME TO BED! -"

-" IT'S ALL RIGHT, HE'S JUST WORRIED ABOUT ME...."-

"WELL, HOW WAS IT FOR YOU?"

-"HAVE YOU EVER THOUGHT OF GETTING YOUR EYES TESTED....."-

"NO, I'M NOT TURNED ON BY ARMOR, I JUST WANT TO BE
SAFE FROM SOCIALLY AND SEXUALLY CONTRACTED DISEASES!"—

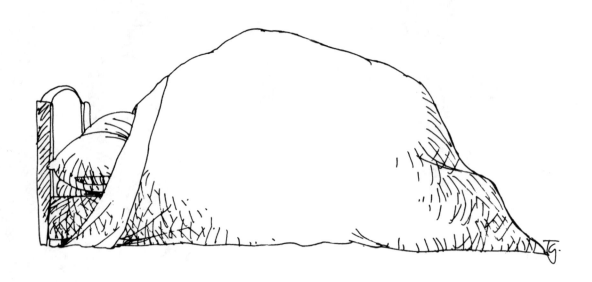

- " OH DAMN! THE BATTERY'S RUN OUT! " -

" ARTHUR, THE DOG'S LAUGHING AGAIN.....'"-

"- WELL IF HE'S NOT YOUR FRIEND, WHOSE FRIEND IS HE?"-

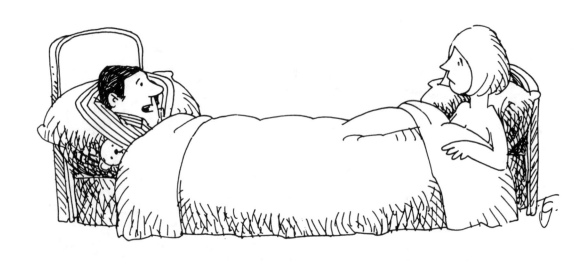

"WELL, IS OUR TRIAL SEPARATION WORKING OUT OR ISN'T IT?"

" I SUPPOSE THIS IS JUST ANOTHER SORDID LITTLE AFFAIR TO YOU, GEORGE. "

"YOU'LL BE PLEASED TO HEAR, ANGELA, THAT I AM NOW AT ONE WITH THE UNIVERSE!"-

" — NOT IN THE PIANO AGAIN, CEDRIC, YOU KNOW I'M NOT MUSICAL!"—

" WELL, YOU TRY FITTING AN AFFAIR IN BETWEEN
SHOPPING AND THE VETS ....."-

-" I DON'T THINK YOU UNDERSTAND WHAT'S MEANT BY
'WIFE-SWAPPING', MR.HARGRAVES !"-

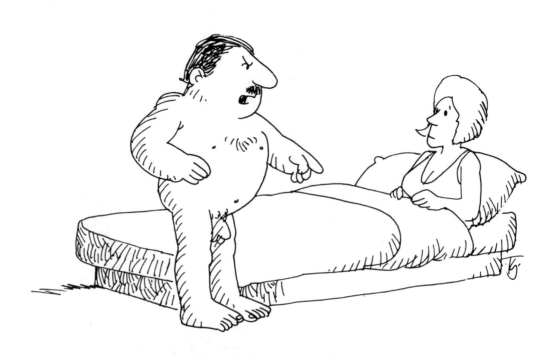

-"WELL, I USUALLY SLEEP ON THAT SIDE IN MY HOME!"-

-"THAT'S A COINCIDENCE, NEITHER DOES MY WIFE'S EXHUSBAND'S LOVER'S GIRLFRIEND..."-

-" IT'S NOT WHAT YOU THINK, HILDA!"-

" - MY WIFE'S JUST LEFT ME !... " -

" AFTERTHOUGHT? NO, AFTER SEX ACTUALLY ", -

–" THE COMPUTER SAYS ' TONIGHT'S THE NIGHT.' "–

"WELL, IF IT HURTS YOUR BACK, YOU SHOULDN'T DO IT!".

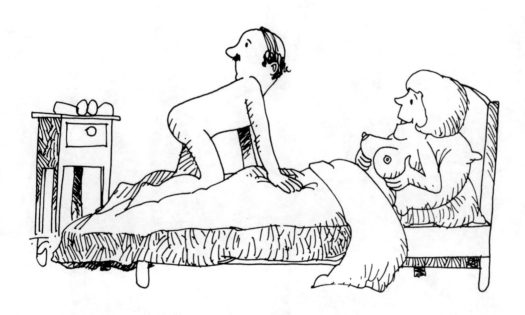

- " YOU DON'T NEED YOUR GLASSES, WE HAVE A BRAILLE SITUATION HERE. "-

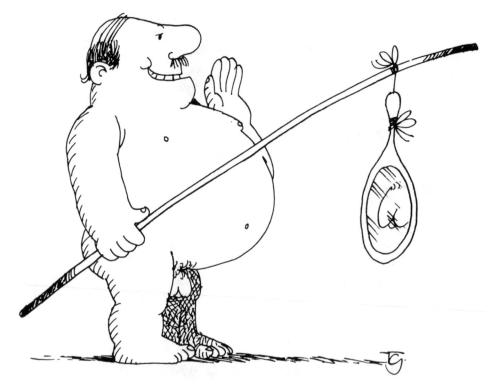

"HELLO THERE, LONG TIME NO SEE ......"-

"A FINE FIGURE OF <u>TWO</u> MEN, I'D SAY....."-

"WELL, I SEE <u>SOMETHING</u> UNDER THERE, IN THE SHADOWS." —

"THERE MUST BE _ONE_ WE COULD TRY?"-

"GEORGE, IT SAYS HERE, THAT NORMAL COUPLES DO IT, **AT LEAST ONCE A WEEK!**" –

" ARE YOU GOING TO SLEEP, OR DO YOU WANT TO FOOL AROUND?"

-"I STILL GET THE URGE, BUT I CAN'T REMEMBER
WHAT FOR....." -

"DO YOU REMEMBER BED BEFORE TELEVISION?"

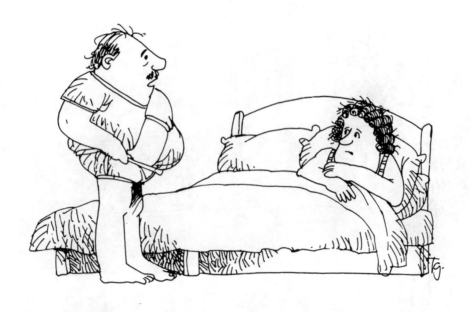

" YOU MEAN, IT'S NOT SEXY TO TUCK MY T-SHIRT
INTO MY UNDERPANTS?" –

"OH NO, NOT MORE OF YOUR APHRODISIAC OYSTERS, EMILY?"

- "WOW! WHAT A GREAT PROGRAM. NOW, WHAT WERE WE DOING?" -

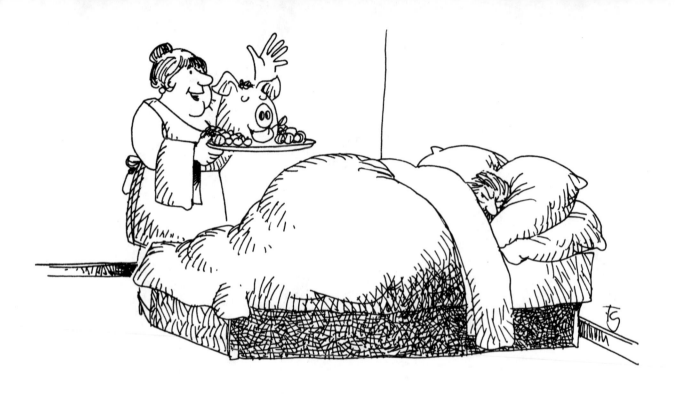

" AWAKE, MY LOVE, HEREWITH A BREAKFAST FIT FOR A
LOVER SUCH AS THOU....." -

-" YOUR 'GO-FOR-IT' HAS 'GONE-FOR-IT'!"-

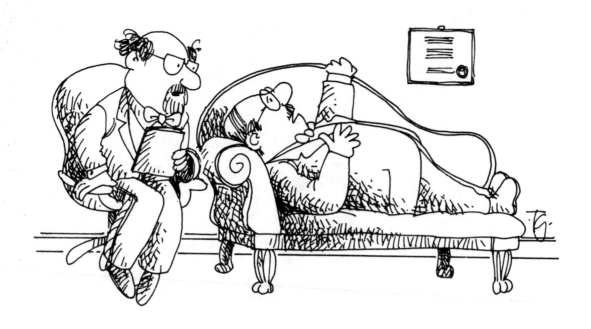

–"I'M GETTING TOO OLD FOR A MID-LIFE CRISIS"–

- " LOVE AND PEACE TO ALL WITHIN......" -

"I KNOW YOU THINK I'M FRIGID, FRANK, BUT THAT IS NOT FUNNY!"

-"AH, I SEE WE'RE BACK TO SEXY CARDIGANS AGAIN......."-

- " I LIKED YOU BETTER, WHEN THAT BULGE
WAS IN YOUR TROUSERS." -

"JOHN, COULDN'T WE DO 'HOBBIES' ANOTHER NIGHT?"

" ROMANCE IS NOT DEAD...."-

"YOU REMEMBER ME, WILLIAM? I USED TO 'GET YOU'
IN THE BIKE SHED AT SCHOOL!"-

-" WELL, I'D LIKE TO RE-LIVE <u>MY</u> YOUTH IN A WARM HOTEL ROOM."-

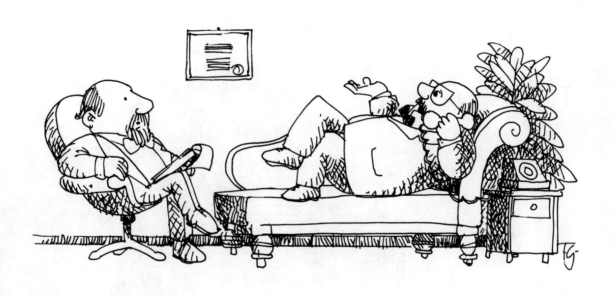

"I DON'T HAVE TIME FOR A MID-LIFE CRISIS!"

"WHEN IT COMES TO SEX, GEORGE HAS NOTHING TO SAY." -

"AH, DOES RESTING UP ON A SATURDAY AFTERNOON, MEAN YOU'LL BE FRESH AND READY TO SEDUCE ME TONIGHT?" –

-" GROUP SEX IS SOMETHING I'VE ALWAYS WANTED TO GET INTO." -

- " I THINK I'VE FORGOTTEN HOW TO DO THIS......" -

" WELL DEAR, YOU CAN STILL MANAGE IT — EVEN AT YOUR AGE....." -

" HE'S BEEN DEEPLY DISTURBED, SINCE HIS 40th BIRTHDAY! "

" I HAVEN'T LEFT YOU, YOU IDIOT!
I'VE JUST BEEN **SHOPPING**!!"

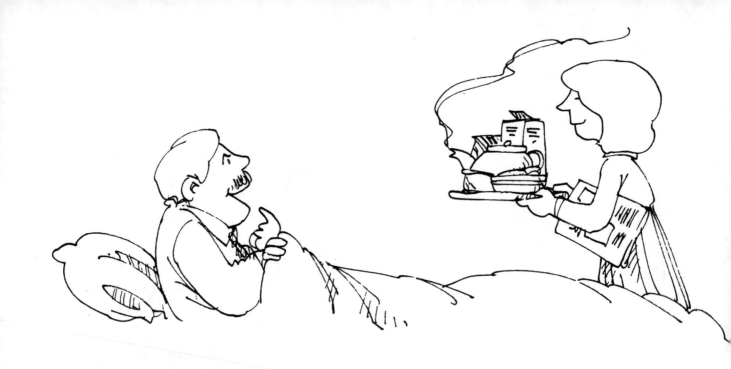

"BREAKFAST IN BED! WOW! THAT MEANS THAT I'VE FORGOTTEN SOMETHING I DID LAST NIGHT OR I SHOULD REMEMBER TO DO SOMETHING TONIGHT......'

"HERE'S YOUR BREAKFAST, TIGER!....."

"AH SEX, YES, I REMEMBER THAT!"

-"I STILL JOG .... DOWN TO THE PUB!"-

." IF HE WAS RIGID , I WOULDN'T BE FRIGID".

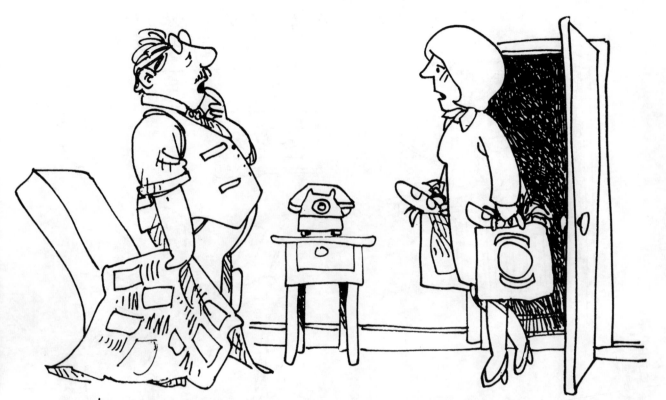

"I CAN'T REMEMBER THE NAME OF WHOEVER IT WAS PHONED ASKING YOU ABOUT SOMETHING OR OTHER .... IMPORTANT.'"

"DID YOU REMEMBER TO TAKE THE DOG OUT FOR HIS WALK TODAY?".

"YOU KNOW WHAT I MISS, ZELDA? TRYING TO DO THIS QUIETLY, SO NOT TO WAKE THE CHILDREN...."

-"ASK MY WIFE TO PASS THE SALT, PLEASE!"-

"HAVE YOU EVER BEEN UNFAITHFUL TO ME, HILDA?"

"THAT WAS A MIND BLOWING DOCUMENTARY, N'EST PAS?".

"COMING TO BED EARLY TONIGHT WAS A GREAT IDEA — SARAH!!" —

"AH, IT'S GOOD TO GET AWAY FROM ALL THAT SEX AND DRUGS AND ROCK AND ROLL FOR A WHILE ISN'T IT DEAR?"

"OH WE'RE INTO GARDENING, WINEMAKING AND GROUP SEX ...."

OTHER GREAT BOOKS BY BOSTON AMERICA

The fine, cultivated stores carrying our books really get ticked if you buy directly from the publisher so if you can, please patronize your local store and let them make a buck. If, however, the fools don't carry a particular title, you can order them from us for $7, postpaid. Credit cards accepted for orders of 4 or more books.

#2400 How To Have Sex On Your Birthday
Finding a partner, special birthday sex positions, kinky sex and much more

#2403 The Good Bonking Guide
Bonking is a very useful British term for "you know what" and this book covers bonking in the dark, bonking all night long, improving your bonking and everything else you might want to know.

#2419 Cucumbers Are Better Than Men Because...
Cucumbers never go soft in a second, aren't afraid of commitment and never criticize.

#2423 Is There Sex After 40
It says normal couples do it at least once a week, you get the urge but can't remember what for and "if he was rigid I wouldn't be frigid".

#2424 Is There Sex After 50
Swapping him for two 25 year olds, being into gardening, wine making and group sex and liking it better when the bulge was in his trousers.

#2430 Is There Sex After 30
Being too tired to get it up, thinking kinky is leaving the lights on and remembering when you could do it 3 times a night.

#2432 Big Weenies
Big weenies and small weenies and all their names and how to find big weenies in a strange town and how to rate them.

#2434 Sex and Marriage
Wives wanting foreplay and romance and husbands wanting to be allowed to go to sleep right after. Techniques for improving your wife or husband or ignoring them.

#2438 Dog Farts
Dogs get blames for lots of farts they don't do but this book gives all the real ones like the sleeping dog fart and the living room fart.

#2446 The PMS Book
This book covers all the problems from irritability to clumsiness to chocolate craving to backaches in a funny and sympathetic manner.

#2450 How To Pick Up Girls
This book holds the keys to understanding women and teaches never fail lines plus places to meet shy, drunk weird and even naked girls

#2451 How To Pick Up Guys
5How to get them to grovel at your feet and how to spot the losers and how to get rid of them after sex.

#2453 Beginners Sex Manual
Covers basics such as how to tell if you're a virgin and good things to say before and after sex.

#2455 Unspeakably Rotten Cartoons
Words cannot describe this totally tasteless and crass collection of cartoons that are guaranteed to offend and make you laugh.

#2457 Hooters
This is a photo book of the latest lingo for boobs and bosoms and bulging breasts.

#2458 Adult Connect The Dots
If you can count and use a pencil at the same time you too can be a pornographer.

#2463 Butts and Buns
These photos take a racy, rear view at women's tushes, beautiful buns and delicate derri

#2465 Do It Yourself Guide To Safe Sex
Well if you do it yourself you can get it right the first time and never catch any nasty disea

#2466 Guide To Intimate Apparel
Photos and purposes of all the lacy lingerie and unmentionables from bloomers to garters wedgies.

#2469 Hunks
A list of all the popular men's names and how they compare in bed and boardroom and physical sizes,

#2470 How To Find A Man And Get Married In 30 Days
Reserve the hall first and then learn ways and places to meet men, how to use sex and h to get rid of your mistakes.

#2471 Student Guide To Farting
The roommate fart, the math teacher fart, the lunch lady fart. This book covers them all.

#2472 Party Games For 30 Year Olds
New racy games and lists of old favorites. This book has them all and will keep a party of year olds going all night.

#2473 Party Games For 40 Year Olds
Similar to the 30 year old book with perhaps more emphasis on sex rather than drinking.

#2474 Party Games For 50 Year Olds
Just like the 30 and 40 year old games but this book gives instruction on keeping the play awake after 10 PM

#2501 Cowards Guide To Body Piercing
Cartoons and explanations of all the good and horrible places you can put holes in yours

#2502 Toilet Tips
Urinal etiquette and handling warm toilet seats or doors with lousy locks or smells that are your own. A must for anyone that uses toilets.

#2503 Kinky World Records
Like the world's hairiest armpits or thickest condom or shortest male organ or longest time take off a bra. Hey, you could set your own records.

#2504 Pregnant Woman's Guide To Farting
The Claustrophobia Fart and the Waiting Room Fart and the Naming the Baby Fart and th Constipation Fart are just a few.

BOSTON AMERICA C★O★R★P

125 Walnut Street, Watertown, MA 02172 (617) 923-1111 FAX: (617) 923-8839